# 2x2=Boo!

## A Set of Spooky Multiplication Stories

written and illustrated by

## Loreen Leedy

Holiday House · New York

For Regina,
who likes the spider chandelier

Library of Congress Cataloging-in-Publication Data
Leedy, Loreen.
2 × 2 = boo! : a set of spooky multiplication stories / written
and illustrated by Loreen Leedy. — 1st ed.
p.    cm.
ISBN 0-8234-1190-7
1. Multiplication—Juvenile literature.   [1. Multiplication.]
I. Title.
QA115.L443        1995        94-46711        CIP        AC
512.2'13—dc20
ISBN 0-8234-1272-5 (pbk.)

# Contents

# The Disappearing Zero

Well, Jinks can multiply, too. Two huge bats grabbed me last week, so she cried:

2×0 = 0!

Get it? Two bats times ZERO equals ZERO bats.

Big deal. Three angry snakes were chasing us, so Griselda yelled:

3×0 = 0!

See? Three snakes times ZERO equals ZERO snakes.

# One More Time

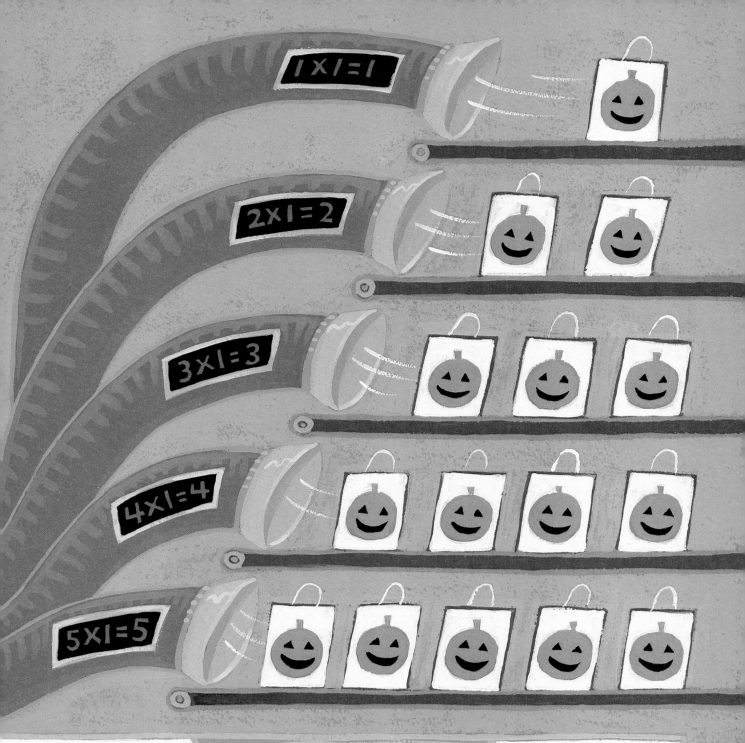

So, I can start with ONE bag of candy, then multiply it by the number of bags I want? Let's try a big number like 99!

Wait, the machine is rumbling, it's going to . . .

# CHAPTER 2

# Seeing Double

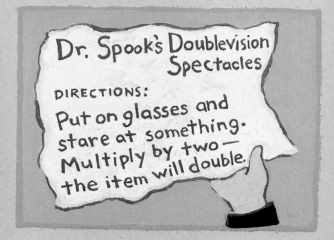

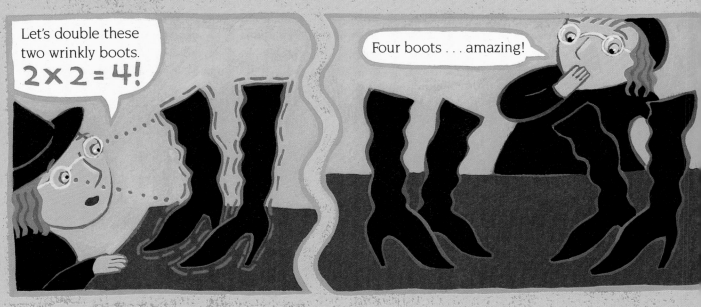

# Triple Scare

CAW! CAW! CAW! CAW!

Help! A giant crow!

Well done, Riley.

20

# Foursight

# Boo Stew

It's perfect, Mr. Bones! You're a genius.

Why thank you, Mrs. Tibia.

1×0=0   2×0=0   3×0=0   4×0=0   5×0=0

Any number times ZERO will equal ZERO.

That's for sure.

1×1=1   2×1=2   3×1=3   4×1=4   5×1=5

Any number times one will equal that number.

Even a really *big* number.

1×2=2   2×2=4   3×2=6   4×2=8   5×2=10

You can double any number by multiplying it by TWO.

You can double any number by multiplying it by TWO.

$1 \times 3 = 3$  $2 \times 3 = 6$  $3 \times 3 = 9$  $4 \times 3 = 12$  $5 \times 3 = 15$

To triple a number, just multiply it by THREE.

$1 \times 4 = 4$  $2 \times 4 = 8$  $3 \times 4 = 12$  $4 \times 4 = 16$  $5 \times 4 = 20$

If I multiply by FOUR, I get four times as much.

Don't touch those cookies.

$1 \times 5 = 5$  $2 \times 5 = 10$  $3 \times 5 = 15$  $4 \times 5 = 20$  $5 \times 5 = 25$

Here are the FIVE desserts for tonight.

EEEK! I love scream puffs.

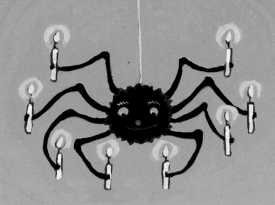

| X | 1 | 2 | 3 | 4 | 5 |
|---|---|---|---|---|---|
| 1 | 1 | 2 | 3 | 4 | 5 |
| 2 | 2 | 4 | 6 | 8 | 10 |
| 3 | 3 | 6 | 9 | 12 | 15 |
| 4 | 4 | 8 | 12 | 16 | 20 |
| 5 | 5 | 10 | 15 | 20 | 25 |

Now that's what I call a multiplication table!